A Collection of Ghost Poetry

Tom Guldin

Published by Tom Guldin, 2024.

A COLLECTION OF GHOST POETRY

First edition. December 1, 2024.

Copyright © 2024 Tom Guldin.

ISBN: 979-8227344342

Written by Tom Guldin.

Table of Contents

Gravedigger's Shadow

The ghostly specter makes his rounds
his shovel still in hand.

In life he dug the graves for all
and toils still in death.

With ghostly hands, still digging graves
though dead for countless years.

He buries secrets and misdeeds
of living and the dead.

He hides the whispers, sins and lies
in ground both dark and deep.

While watchful spirits linger near
awoken from their sleep.

Introduction

Most of the poems in this collection are ghost poems taking place primarily in a graveyard setting. Some of these are somber, reflecting a sadness and melancholy in those departed spirits. Others are light and comedic. But there are a few reflecting how a spirit could become vengeful under certain circumstances. These poems are stand-alone poems and as such can be read in any order.

The poems grouped under *The Ghost's Lament* are of a different sort. This series of poems constitute a Novel(Short Story?)-in-Verse and feature fragmented moments of a ghost haunting an old house, and her efforts to interact with the new owners. Through this series of snapshots, the poems embrace themes of loneliness, loss and finally acceptance. The characters in these poems — whether ghostly or alive — are intimately tied to the house. The range of poems reflect how these characters come to terms with the inevitable conclusion.

As a Novel-in-Verse, the poems as designed to tell a complete story with a Beginning, Middle and End and are designed to be read sequentially. Each poem can be read and enjoyed as a stand-alone poem, however to receive the full benefits of the story they should be read sequentially.

A Note on Formatting

This is a book of poetry designed to be read in lines of verse, for the most part. Some of the poems, however, are of a form known as *prosimetrum* which is a form that combines both prose and verse. The poems *The Last Note* and *The Visitor Between Sleep* are example of this type of poem and consist of a segment of prose followed by a verse poem designed to enhance the prose.

Ghost of the Forgotten Staircase

She drifts along forgotten stairs
in shadows deep where silence hangs,
the ghostly bride with windswept veil.

Her alluring spectral grace
illuminated through moonlit panes,
she haunts these halls of time's decay.

Bound in twilight's floating light
forever lost, she roams alone
her sorrow lingers, year to year.

She speaks no sound
yet faded song beneath her breath
intones of memories, deep and old.

Come listen now as tales unfold
of memories bound by ancient will,
the shroud of stories she cannot let go.

Part 1: Ghost Poems

Whispers of Forgotten Souls

In the folds of mist
twilight hides its secrets,
and somewhere in the distance
footsteps drift on the wind.

As if from another world
a memory of forgotten souls
rises unbidden through thinned veils
and the breeze speaks of those long gone

The Thinning Veil

On All Hallow's Eve
when veils between worlds grow thin
spirits slowly rise —
seeking one who might just catch,
cries of longing in the dark.

A lone specter glides by —
wishing on the breeze
"Is there one to bravely hear,
just one soul with whom to share the joy."

Glows softly flicker
from carved pumpkins lighting the way,
yet laughter feels far
for those who drift and whisper
so softly from the shadows

Lonely spirits long
to share laughter, dance and words
dreaming of lost friends
and souls to share old stories —
Just one heart to listen close.

The Last Note

They told me the old theater had been closed for years, ever since the final performance — the one that ended in silence. The pianist, a brilliant yet troubled soul, collapsed mid-piece, his notes fading unfinished into the dusty air. No one returned after that, those who did claimed they could hear him still playing after hours. But ghost stories never keep me away.

I sneak into the darkened theater, the scent of mildew clinging to the red velvet curtains, rows of seats face a stage veiled in shadow. I walk closer to the grand piano at center stage, ignoring the chill racing up my spine. Then I hear it — a single note. A chord, trembling softly into the air, echoing long past its life. My breath catches. The room feels impossibly large, like something ancient is holding its breath.

The keys begin to depress on their own, one by one, the piece slowly rebuilding itself, as if coaxing life from silence. I listen in awe, but also in terror. It's beautiful, haunting, the kind of music that calls to the deepest parts of me. But this song shouldn't exist, not anymore.

Through the dust-flecked beams of moonlight, I glimpse his hand hovering above the keys — transparent and faded.

a song unfinished
lingers in this vacant hall—
why do you return?
each night you play for the lost,
and I come to listen too

The Visitor Between Sleep

I wake drenched in sweat, the echo of my own footsteps still in my ears, and a faint scent of something burning. A dream shouldn't linger this long, shouldn't follow me into the day like a shadow.

This time, when I wake, I hear the door. A soft creak—my bedroom door, opening slowly like it does in the dream. But I'm alone. Aren't I? The room feels wrong, too cold, the air too thin. I see a footprint pressed into the carpet, wet and muddy. I haven't been outside, not since the afternoon. I remind myself this is just the aftershock of sleep. It has to be. But then comes the whisper—closer now.

I call out in a voice that quivers more than I'd like. No reply... just breathing. Not mine.

the boundary between
dreams and waking fades —
you were real, weren't you?
even when you held the dark
and slipped between the shadows

Echoes of Shadows

The air felt thick, heavy with memories of lives long gone. Moonlight filtered through broken windows, casting jagged patterns on the floor. A faint creak sounded from the staircase, but no one stood there. The house breathed, its walls holding secrets, its silence louder than any noise. Cold drafts whispered through the halls, carrying the weight of unseen eyes. Every shadow seemed alive, flickering in and out of existence, as if waiting for something—or someone—to remember they were still there.

Whispers in the dark,
Footsteps echo on cold stone,
Shadows never rest.

The Graveyard Gathering

On Halloween night, the graveyard glowed under a full moon, shadows danced among ancient tombstones. Jack-o'-lanterns flickered with grins, their carved eyes illuminating the multi-hued autumn leaves beneath. Wisps of fog curled around granite markers.

All Hallow's Eve calls out to spirits —
the veil is thinned, the passage open,
as ghostly will-o'-the-wisps - now summoned, rise.

As the clock struck midnight, a faint rustling echoed through the night. Unearthly murmurs arose as spectral figures stirred from their resting places. Ascending, ghostly, intertwining within the tendrils of fog.

Moonlit whispers drift in shadows,
as ghosts all gather for tales of old,
and haunting laughter fills the night.

Grinning jack-o'-lanterns watch and wait
as ghouls and ghosts and other ilk
all gather for shared tales of woe.

Together, they floated gracefully above the hallowed ground, their translucent forms shimmering in the moonlight, eager to share the poignant tales of their demise on this most haunted of nights.

They share their fates, in whispers soft
the echoes of the lives they've lost
as tales of grief, each shade intones.

A heart once full, now empty stands
he tells his tale of love betrayed
and weeps for thoughts of what once was.

A maiden fair all clad in white
long lost upon the stormy seas,
her soft voice now a haunting sigh.

A regal shade, clad in velvet fair,
told of her failed rendezvous
her fateful fall in dark of night.

The spirits looked toward the growing light in the east and to each other.
All Hallow's Eve was drawing to a close and the veil would soon be
closing. The time had come to say farewells and bring the evening's tales
to a close.

With dawning light, they all agree
to return next year by moon's first light,
more tales of sorrow they guarantee.

The Keeper of Lost Souls

Drifting between the shadowed trees, voicing her soft lullaby,
a keeper of the weary dead, beneath the watchful midnight skies.

Guarding those who restless roam, the darkened graveyards all alone
they walk the nights to find repose, their thoughts on how they could
atone.

Her whispers calm these haunted souls, that shiver in the black of night,
urging peace beneath the stars, for specters searching for the light.

A shepherd for those lonely ones, who could not find the way to cross,
those doomed souls who wander here and seek release from mortal loss.

The Lantern Bearer

The Lantern Bearer walks alone, a beacon in the dark
his light guides those weary souls, with gentle, ghostly spark.

Forlorn spirits who wander still, in graveyards where their bodies lie,
and seek release from earthly bounds that will not let them go.

Each has their reason to walk alone, lost love or mission left unfilled,
and search for meaning in the night, their wistful cries for naught.

The flickering light — a sign of hope, that calls to spirits alone and lost
and with his light they drift to peace from earth at last set free.

Haiku

creaking doors invite
whispers forgotten in the past —
shadows flicker past

in the gloom murmurs
hearing secrets from the walls...
ghosts dance in the dust

chill in the air
echoes of laughter linger...
unseen hands brush close

The Phantom Piper

In mist shrouded night, the lonesome music echoes amid darkened graves. The spectral piper weaves a ghostly strain, luring the lost spirits from their earthly tombs. His haunting melody reminding the dead of lives they once lived.

The piper's tune at midnight sounds
a haunting, lilting plea.

His notes a bridge from earth to sky
to set lost spirits free.

Gravestones tremble, touched by song
as mournful voices sing,

and phantoms rise on trembling notes
that forlorn refrains bring.

For Debbie who is always there for me.

The Weeping Woman

The aging cherub covered headstone leans,
reflection of the mother's grief.
Caught between her love, her loss,
tethered to this darkened grave.

She weeps beside the nameless stone
her grief, each night, laid bare.
Her wails drift through haunted night,
soft whispers in the air.

Chained by love, by loss profound,
she haunts this hallowed space.
Her sorrow deep, a hollow sound
that time cannot erase.

The Silent Choir

The choir's voice, so faint, so fair
a background murmur in the night,
a haunting beauty to those who hear.

Its otherworldly echoed hymns,
sings of remembrance, of farewell,
that floats across the graves.

The silent choir fills the night
with song so soft, so sweet,
each voice a whisper from the past,

where memories both ebb and flow.
A song to ease the souls that hear
before eternal sleep.

The Forgotten Names

The nameless graves lie cold and dark,
forgotten through the years.

Neglected by all living kin,
unkept and overgrown.

These restless spirits wander far
for some acknowledgement.

Their spirits drift like autumn mist,
with quiet, unseen tears.

They wait for voices, lost in time
to speak their names once more

and hope that wistful memories
will find them as before.

The Graveyard Gatekeeper

He guards the border 'tween life and death
the spectral graveyard keeper.

Bound as he is to watch the gate
a guardian of the boarder,

he must decide which souls may pass
a task he will not shirk.

Each night with eyes of burning coals
he watches spirits move,

and silently he turns them back
or opens paths unknown.

A noiseless sentinel he stands
forever bound — alone.

The Weary Watcher

The watcher stands with quiet eyes
a guard through countless years.

'Tis love or duty that binds them here,
they mark the boundless years.

They linger still, a ghostly form
pledged through the endless years.

Their love holds fast, beyond compare
though all the countless years.

The Haunting Fog

The graveyard sits in chill of night
as ghostly fog rolls in.

Like spectral hands that reach and grasp
the fog creeps low and sure.

It's wisps have thoughts, regrets and loss
alive within its swirls

and carry whispers soft and cold
like autumn's final blast.

Each wisp a tale, of loss or woe
dissolved in soft cold mist

and secrets hang in midnight air
from loved ones that are missed.

The Tolling Bell

A midnight bell tolls in the dark
it serves to raise the dead

a call to gather all lost souls
who by this sound are led.

None know who nightly rings the bell
and specters can not tell

but sound it does this haunting knell
a voice from far beyond

and spirits drift on soft mist coils
to gather and respond.

The Mirror Pool

For years people would tell me of the Mirror Pool in the graveyard. That after a long autumn shower would fill the stone basin and the full moon shone overhead, you could see loved ones long departed gazing back at you...if you stared long enough. But their stories came with a warning as well...

In waters still, reflections of faces long gone,
a ghostly mirror deep and dark and clear.
Where souls stare back from under glass,
with haunting pleading eyes.
A glimpse of death for those who dare,
to look on darkened need.

The Cursed Crypt

Dark and malevolent, the crumbling crypt had stood for longer than any could remember. Even the cemetery keepers had no recollection of when it was built or, more importantly, who was buried there. The name chiseled into the granite face had long since worn away and even the symbols, dark arcane symbols, surrounding the iron door had been worn by time's ravages. Local lore had it that those who entered, never returned.

No light can reach
who enters there,
though whispers lure them on.

Like dark on dark,
cursed visions twist
with shadows deep, profound.

Each step a path
to endless night
where sound and light are gone

and those that dare
to venture in
are never to be found.

The Grave of the Forgotten

A soul, a ghost, lies here alone
left to molder by those dear.

No stone, no name, no tear was shed
for the solitary soul left here.

Its hatred now has turned to rage
as hard as graveyard stone.

With hollow cries, it screams and wails
and lashes out in wrath

at any soul who wanders close
and chances in their path.

The Cry of the Raven

In the hush of midnight's veil,
the mournful raven wails
like a lost child's cry echoing through the graveyard,
its wings slice the thick air, shadowy and pale.

Hovering above the resting dead,
a sentinel of sorrow, it watches them,
as if each headstone whispers secrets
only it can understand.

While moonlight bathes the silent ground,
setting a stage for life and death,
as echoes shape the way we mourn,
and souls take wing at night.

With a caw that curls through darkness deep,
it stirs the spirits from their slumber,
like the mist rising from the earth,
thick and haunting, swirling in unison.

The spirits heed its cry,
from graves where shadows creep.
and rise like mist in sorrow's shroud,
a dance of ghostly breath.

As they emerge, woven in twilight,
their stories slipping through the cracks of time,
a communion of memories and lingering sighs,
floating like dust in the night's embrace.

The Haunted Willow

In the solemn quiet of the graveyard,
the willow bows heavy with grief,
its branches dripping with the weight of tears,
like sorrow spilling from ancient lips.

Each leaf unfurls with a mournful face
that echoes a once vibrant life, now trapped
in the gnarled embrace of time,
clinging to the tree as memories cling to the wind.

The willow holds secrets deep within its core,
a tapestry woven of longing, loss, sorrow,
tales draped in shadow,
a graveyard's heart, hanging with whispered prayers.

Softly weeping, the willow remembers,
cradling those who drift like mist,
its roots entwined with the remnants of souls,
an intimate bond, profound and eternal.

The Collector of Souls

The Collector roams the midnight graveyard,
a phantom cloaked in darkness,
an inky, black shadow against the night
his lantern glowing like a hungry eye,
searching the quiet for lost souls to devour.

The lantern's flicker, dancing like a candle
guttering in the wind beckons to the unwary
drawing them into the depths of night
to trap all remnants of life.

Each captured soul, becomes a fading spark,
pulled into his glassy prison,
their essence swirling like smoke,
lost to the suffocating darkness.

The lantern, now a graveyard's heart,
beats with quiet, sinister pulses,
where echoes of final cries are quelled,
silenced in the cold embrace of despair.

Each lantern's pulse holds secrets,
the weight of countless souls,
each a story untold, a life extinguished,
forever wandering the edges of oblivion.

In the stillness, the Collector waits,
eternal, hungry, an unending harvest,
his shadow stretching with the twilight,

a promise whispered among the restless graves.

The Night of Lost Dreams

The night of dreams long lost arrives
in sighs of silvered mist,
a veil draws over the graveyard,
as shadows waltz with memories.

Each ghost recalls the lives unlived,
loves they never kissed, paths they never took,
each whisper a tender lament,
a symphony of "if onlys."

Unfinished melodies drift around,
tangled in threads of unspoken words,
murmuring soft of hopes long past,
the weight of lives they couldn't live.

In this mournful gathering,
they live again in fleeting moments,
each memory a flickering candle
snuffed out before its time could shine.

Their silent dreams, a fragile offering
to the stars, lingers like a soft caress,
lost forever, yet eternally alive
within the whisper of the night.

The Candle in the Crypt

A candle flickers in the tomb,
its yellow flame a beacon to the lost,
flickering in this vault of shadows,
where time intertwines with sorrow.

No hand to light, no breath to blow,
yet still it ever burns,
an enigma drawing whispers
from the depths of night.

A spark of life in endless dark,
where only silence grows,
it sways to the rhythm of forgotten dreams,
etching lines of longing on the walls.

The souls gather, drawn like moths,
their forms shimmering in the dimness,
memories wrapped in layers of grief,
wishes tangled in the threads of fate.

The candlelight beckons,
guiding them to relive the moments,
the laughter unspoken, the promises unmet,
each flicker igniting a memory anew.

The Phantom Lover

I.

A phantom lover stands alone beside the marble tomb,
the echoes of a heartbeat faint, yet deeply felt within,
they speak of love that time forgot, lost amid the gloom,
where shadows dance and memories whisper of what has been.

Each sigh escapes like softest wind, caressing ancient stone,
the weight of longing clings like ivy, binding spirits near,
their whispers reach the cold, still earth, like tears that cannot dry,
in hopes one day their love might join and rise into the sky.

Yet every star that lights the night reminds of distance vast,
for moments lost are prisms warped, refracting all their pain,
with every breath, a thousand dreams unraveling too fast,
the curse of love that binds the soul, a bond they cannot feign.

As twilight falls, their heart takes flight, to bridge the void of fate,
with whispered vows that linger, united soon, though late.

II.

Upon this hallowed ground they stand, where silence speaks of grief,
a tether drawn through realms unseen, where time no longer weeps.
In shadows thick, they weave their thoughts, entwined with sweet belief,
that love can pierce the fabric dark, through dreams that fate still keeps.

Each whispered word a fragile thread, connecting heart to heart,
regrets spill forth like petals lost, crushed gently by the night.
Yet in their strength, the hopes ignite, refusing to depart,
for love transcends the bounds of death, and flickers with soft light.

As moonlight bathes the grave in silver, kindred spirits yearn,
the promise of a sweet embrace, a longing deep and true,
and though together they can not be, their hearts they still do burn,
they vow to seek in realms beyond, a bond forever new.

So here beside the tomb they stand, in sighs of love's refrain,
till time shall yield and souls unite, to bloom beyond the pain.

The Riddle of the Graves

The graves speak in riddles deep,
in carvings faint and sly,
etchings that tangle like roots beneath the surface,
whispers of the past drifting in the evening air.

Their hidden words a puzzle cast,
for seekers who pass by,
each headstone a guardian of secrets unspoken,
echoes of lives intertwined with the whispering wind.

They beckon with shadows, inviting inquiry,
each epitaph a breadcrumb, leading nowhere...
yet somewhere. In the fractured silence,
the truth waits, patient and elusive.

The living pause, squinting at the stone,
trying to decipher the meaning,
their hearts aching for connections,
as the ground listens, holding its breath.

While faintly laughter echoes
as spirits dance beyond the veil,
delighted by the quest they've posed,
reminder that the dead still see, still speak.

The Manor

Deep in the heart of a gloom-shrouded moor,
where veils between worlds grow thin and elusive,
the manor rises through a miasmic mist.
Shadows, like ephemeral serpents, twist,
curling in ethereal tangles birthing sinister curses.

A lonesome sentinel abandoned by the world,
its worn visage a testament to time's unyielding tyranny,
it carries the collective sorrows of generations long gone.
Whispers, like tendrils of sorcery,
permeate the fetid air, seductive power
coiling around unsuspecting souls.

Within the bowels of this accursed place,
a melancholic symphony of lost hopes.
Forgotten dreams permeate the atmosphere,
the manor's tortured inhabitants,
caught in the spectral dances of anguish,
silently beseech for a release that may never come.

Whispers of forgotten voices
drift like tattered remnants of a bygone era,
timeworn echoes seeping through the cracks,
frail specters trapped in perpetual torment.
Malevolence, like an ancient specter
coils within the darkness,
weaving its secrets through unearthly murmurs.

Each haunting wail that resonates,

an embrace of despair,
forlorn cries of souls trapped in eternal anguish.
They yearn for redemption, seeking solace
in depths where darkness reigns,
and shadows writhe and secrets slumber.
A realm where the essence of redemption
entwines within a fathomless abyss.

Haunted by insatiable longing,
tormented specters hunger for the forbidden caress
of a wayward wanderer, flickering, ghostly forms
with a desperate craving. They sway
in the shadow's oppressive embrace
seeking to break free from the suffocating curse.
Phantom limbs outstretched
towards a glimmer of elusive hope.

Cursed spirits thirsting not for mere respite,
but for rapturous dreams, a fleeting taste,
liberation, forever out of reach.
Forlorn apparitions trapped in a macabre dance,
they writhe and twist, an incorporeal presence,
shadows on the fringes of mortal perception.
A lamentation echoing the manor's sorrowful whispers.

A wanderer emerges, an anomaly
in a forsaken, melancholic landscape.
He steps into the desolation,
an unsettling aura descends,
a manifestation of ancient cosmic forces
tugging at the fabric of reality.

Whispers, once filled with longing,
transformed into an unholy chorus,
voices of the trapped spirits twisted by deep malevolence.
The manor's lament resonates with a newfound intensity,
an echo reverberating through the fabric of existence.
The spirits, instead of finding redemption,
become entwined in a web of madness,
consumed by ancient, incomprehensible forces.

The ethereal veil unravels within the desolate moor,
now a malignant gateway,
shadows writhe and contort,
entwining with the wanderer,
assimilating him into the maddening, nightmare symphony.
Boundaries, once separating realms, collapse,
crumbling under the weight of an insidious darkness,
overpowering hope's feeble efforts,
the twisted echoes of the manor's whispers reverberate.
Unyielding testament to the power of dormant terrors
that lie enshrouded within the forsaken realm.

Part 2: The Ghost's Lament

Chapter 1: Haunting

The Whispering Door

The old mansion at the end of the lane was long forgotten, its windows like hollow eyes watching for those careless enough to approach. As children, we would dare each other to climb the crumbling steps, but none of us were brave enough to linger. The door always seemed slightly ajar—inviting, as though the house itself had secrets it longed to share. Tonight, I stand before it again, the cold air biting at my neck, feeling drawn to something I can't explain.

Inside, the air feels thick with memories. Every old floorboard whines beneath my weight, but something else moves here—quiet, but unmistakable. The temperature drops sharply, and I hear it, that soft, impossible whisper. They're near. They've always been near.

flickering ghost-light,
a face turns in the darkness —
those eyes, like mine,
searching through midnight rooms
for something we've both forgotten

Breath on Glass

whispers in shadows...
apologetic spirits
haunt stark bare halls
no frills needed to convey
the chill of ancient regrets

I move through these rooms like a shadow slipped from the edges of a forgotten evening. I have no name here, no solid form that time itself could recognize. The walls do not greet me. The stairs do not creak beneath the weight of my presence. Yet I linger. My touch on the air is a whisper, a shiver, a draft from nowhere. I try to remind the house that I was here—that I still am here—but the mirrors stay blank, the floors smooth and untouched. No hollow in the cushions where I once sat, no mark upon the glass where I've stood for hours, tracing the edges of familiar faces now forgotten.

I leave no shadow
and yet the house grows colder—
my breath unreturned,
its silence is louder now
than the life once held within.

The Child's Eyes

In the quiet corners of this house, I find her—small and wide-eyed, glancing beneath the weight of dust and shadow. She moves like a beam of light, where warmth touches the cold. There's a flicker of recognition behind her gaze, a knowing that curls around the edges of her innocence. I hover like a sigh, too softly woven into the fabric of her world. My presence is a story not yet told, lingering in the spaces between her laughter and her fear, as she shivers at the rustle of curtains, at echoes that belong to a time when the house was alive. Does she feel me? Does she sense the echo of longing in these walls, stitched together with memories I can't quite grasp?

How small is the space
between knowing and not?
Her gaze flickers, spark—
a breath held in quiet thrill,
the ghost of connection stirs.

Touch of Wind

In twilight's grip, I drift on wisps of chill,
a phantom's breath that stirs the dust of night.
I sigh against the pane, yet feel no thrill,
for all my whispers fade, just out of sight.

With fingers light, I rattle door and glass,
a fleeting tremor, fleeting as my dream.
The world grows heavy, and my shadows pass,
yet in this silence, only echoes scream.

To touch the warmth of life—what agony!
A candle flickers—then snuffs out like hope.
In longing's grasp, I yearn for memory,
a gentle pulse from which I cannot cope.

I haunt the corners where I dare to tread,
a ghost unheeded, lost, and left for dead.

The New Mother

I love our new home, the old Victorian charm with the filigreed gables. The wood banister showing the years and care of a bygone era. Yes, it stood empty a long time. I like to think it was waiting, waiting for the right family, waiting for us. The dusty corners and cobwebs when we first got here. The first bit of unease at moving in is fading. Jim says it was just stress, the stress of a new move. The kids seem to like the place. Still...there are times it feels like I'm being watched...

She sweeps past me, arms full of the warmth
that once lived in these halls —
I reach out and remember
I can not feel
or be felt.

Echoes of the Night

I am a pulse beneath the floorboards
a sigh between closed doors
In darkness, I bend the house to hear me
but only the child turns her head.

I reach out to her
a soft whisper, a brush of wind —
she glances my way
but her eyes still look through me.

Chapter 2: Remembering

The Mirror's Truth

I follow along, as days turn to weeks, a mere drop in the eternity I have spent waiting. They clean the house, they rearrange the attic uncovering things lost to time — lost even in my memories. The old chest with clothes from a bygone era, clothes I once wore, once loved. The old dusty mirror that was old when I was a child, was in the house before even I arrived, so many years ago.

In the mirror's cracked skin
I catch a flicker —
eyes hollowed out by time
but once...once they held light
behind them

Lover's Chair

This chair held us both
once —
your hand, my hand
touching without thought or fear
of ever letting go.

Now it sits, faded, dusty,
threadbare and worn...discarded
in a corner of the cobwebbed attic
a relic, long forgotten
as I am forgotten.

The First Memory

I see the old photographs as they empty boxes, unable to touch them, I stare over their shoulders. They comment on how things must have been so many years ago...getting most of it wrong. The husband lifts a picture and comments on the stern face, he doesn't know, the picture taken after we'd argued...

I said...something...
sharp, jagged, but your voice —
was it anger? No, regret —
waiting like a storm too quiet to hear
until it was too late.

Gesture of Flowers

I watch from the shadows as flowers bloom in joyful chaos, soft petals carrying whispers of what once was. She reaches for them, a gentle smile curving her lips. A faint scent, elusive, ephemeral, hangs in the air, one my heart remembers. Flowers were an unspoken conversation, a bridge of color, grace, even in silence. The tension of our last words melts away. I longed to speak to you then, to say words of love that hovered like a phantom between us, yet they remained unvoiced, entwined in the petals.

You left flowers
on the table,
the color of forgiveness.
I never said the words—
they hung between us, unspoken.

Sleeping Shadows

In the stillness of night,
I watch them breathe,
the quiet rise and fall
of innocent dreams unbroken—
the new mother curled close,
her child resting like a whisper.

The moon spills silver light
across the floor, painting a delicate line
to where I linger,
my existence woven into the shadows,
humbled but heavy with longing.

I remember, your warmth
melded with mine,
the hum of safe moments,
the rhythm of shared breaths
in a space filled with love,
as we drifted through
the invisible threads of night.

But now, the echo of your laughter
is a ghost behind the veils,
and I remain,
a silhouette in the corner,
a shadow without weight,
watching life unfold without me,
a witness to what was lost—
dreams that no longer caress my heart,

the simple peace we once had,
now a soft ache
that clouds the edges of my mind.

The Child's Hand

In the depths of slumber,
the child stirs,
her small hand reaching out,
fingertips brushing
through the space where I hover,
barely touching,
yet I feel that fleeting spark;
the ache of memory floods me,
and I am lost once more—
in the vastness of what could have been.

Chapter 3: Yearning

The Child's Drawings

Scattered papers cover the table,
crayon lines bursting in color,
as if the world within her mind
has finally spilled out.
Shapes come alive,
fingers grasping at ghosts,
where shadows twist like ribbons,
and laughter echoes, soft,
in crumpled corners of the page.

Each swirl a whisper,
each stroke, a story
she pulls from the depths of dust —
sketches of warmth beneath dark,
bringing to life the space I inhabit,
the light I cannot touch.

"Is this you?" she asks,
her small arm reaching,
fragile as the air,
and I feel the tremor of connection;
I glance over her shoulder,
knowing breath exists
between us,
woven in the colors she lays bare.

I Want to be Seen

In the silence of these crowded rooms, I linger like a half-formed thought, hovering around every creak of floorboards and whisper of wind. The laughter of the living dances past me, yet no one stops to notice the way shadows flicker at the edges, the way my heart aches with wanting. I unravel like string unwound, thrumming with a wish to break through this invisible barrier, to scream, to weep, to connect. But I remain a phantom—a breath, a pulse, untethered, unseen, a longing so deep it aches inside the hollow of my being.

In this room of noise,
I rise on tremors of hope —
a wisp caught in light.
Is it selfish to crave breath,
to dream of being more than air?

The Doorways Between Us

I try means more desperate
to get them to notice
just a look, just a glance
to show they know I am here.

I slam every door,
shake every window,
but it leaves naught but fear
and dread on their faces.

they recoil in horror
at each moving vase
at each cold, chill breeze
at each noise that I make.

In hushed voices they speak
of leaving all behind
but that's not what I want...
to get them to notice
is all that I need.

The Child Speaks

Week after week, I try
I sit with the child
as she plays.
She notices me more,
the parents fear me —
when they acknowledge me at all.
I speak to her in whispers soft
I tell her my name —
sometimes I think she cocks her head
as if listening —
does she hear me?

She says it —
something small, something fragile —
a whisper that barely lifts
into the air.
But I hear it
as though it is a name.

The Moment of Death

The parents continue cleaning
opening rooms long closed,
even to my wanderings.

In one room, toys
a crib, a cradle
the nursery we made
hoping for the day

Overwhelming sadness blankets me
I look at the small vial,
the discarded stopper.

The truth falls like glass —
I was here,
I died here,
waiting for a reason,
for a forgiving word...
a word that never came.

Chapter 4: Letting Go

To Release the House

I know I cannot remain now,
the world of the living
no longer meant for me.

I smile at the new mother,
the child, the family,
this is their time
their house — now.

The walls cannot hold me
anymore —
my hands slip from their icy touch
and I am floating further out
no longer reaching for now.

Dream of the Lost

I look out
a misty veil seems to part
I see her, my child
long gone —

the memory is bittersweet.
I feel the pain,
long held, long cherished,
release —
like the lifting of a great weight.

I understand now
she has moved on
shed the pain of this world,
it is my time.

You come to me
through thinly cast veils
and you say nothing —
but in your eyes, I see
there is no more waiting.

A Parting Gift

I leave behind
a memory
one that was never mine —
a gift for the child
who knew I was there.

A drawing in crayon
a token —
originally hers, embellished
so slightly
for her to remember
a magical time.

Final Goodbye

I accept it now
I must shed these attachments
This mortal world, no longer mine,
it is time to move on
A peaceful acceptance washes over my soul.

I turn from creaking floors,
the wall that carried my whispers
I will not be returning —
I leave nothing behind
only dust and breath.

Into the Wind

I am lighter now
I drift
toward whatever awaits
across the veil.
The world left behind...
behind all the turbulence
ahead release.

I am just a breeze now
nameless, weightless
scattered across the sky.
There is no need for reflection —
only the quiet of leaving.

About the Author

Tom Guldin is a genre writer and poet living in the West Texas panhandle. He's been writing in his spare time for many years. His work has been published or is forthcoming in *Palabras, parABnormal, Scifaikuest,* and the *Whispers from Beyond, Texas Bards, The Drabbun Anthology,* and the *Ghosts, Echoes & Shadows* anthologies.

NOTE: Tom is the one on the left, the one on the right is Her Majesty Amber the First, his cat overlord.